POEts,
MaRTYRS &
SATyRS

NEW AND
SELECTED POEMS:
1959—2001

~~~~~~~~

Jordan Miller

ACADEMY

CHICAGO

Previously published:
Choice: "And Now Winter," "Some Times Before Christmas," "Here Lies Carney"
Gallery Series One/Poets: "For Marjorie," "Mother Among the Philodendra,"
"Painting in an Ale House," "Still Life With Sleep"
Hammers: "Bequest"
Midwest: "Measuring"
Port Chicago Poets: "Poet's Lament," "Elegy for My Father," "The Prize," "The Poet,"
"Poem from the City," "The Children"

Hardcover edition published in 2002 by Lake View Press
Paperback edition published in 2020 by Academy Chicago Publishers
An imprint of Chicago Review Press
814 North Franklin Street
Chicago, Illinois 60616
ISBN 978-1-64160-499-4

Cover design: Sarah Olson
Interior design: Sadie Teper

The Library of Congress has cataloged the hardcover edition as follows:
Miller, Jordan, 1926-
  Poets, martyrs & satyrs : new and selected poems, 1959-2001 / Jordan
Miller
        p. cm.
  ISBN 0-941702-54-5 (hardcover)
  I. Title: Poets, martyrs, and satyrs. II. Title.
  PS3613.I539 P64 2002
  811'.6—dc 21

                                          2002007886

Printed in the United States of America

To Bruce Miller for his constant
encouragement and his invaluable critical advice

Poet's Lament

What can he do with silence?

Battalions of birds
splay their wings
over the limping sea,
thin-lipped horizon
offers only weeds
to rattle on the sand;
a single starfish
makes its mark
underneath the sun,

No bushes to burn
nor rocks to tap,
no trees to drip their gum.

The Prize

"The prostitute, resentful of
being a woman, hates men and
seeks to emasculate them out
of revenge."
                    —Book review

Beyond the roost of thought she lived,
Some lattice-work of impulse moved
her arm, taught her thing to give . . .

Why she chose the life she could not
Say. Oh, the rust of economics
Doubtless played some role, dirty
Streets and hallways, the smell of angry
Onions hissing in the pot . . .

And so she fought upon her bed of pain.
The scissors of her womanhood
Could cut the ardor of the biggest
Men; Medusa-headed monsters
Would spring to life again.

But she grew tired of her crusade:
Her body sagged from battles waged
In cheap hotels beneath the light
Of gasping neon signs that breathed
Through panes; her smiles were hard as gargoyle
Grimaces sculpted deep in stone
As years pinched her flesh to bone.

She watched the men cede their power
To the firmer girls, turning with something
Not too far from lust inside
The narrow pockets of her skin.

In the last lost cause of grief
Her dedication stayed unyielding
As a rock for martyrs must be cold.

Bereft of solid battle tools
She spent her days and nights beguiling
With her lies drunken workmen
on their way to sleep. Alas
for soldiers wearing purple bruises
as their only prize.

And Now Winter

And now, winter. Sunlight pales the air.
Behind our blinded window we cannot tell
What season breaks its art upon the ice.
Thin trees are naked in the morning where
They shake their branches like a muffled bell
Whose tongue is silent with the weight of mice
That skitter on the stranded ropes they tear.
The world has turned a notch, and this cold spell
Holds the frozen liquids in its vice.

Behind our pane which frames the frosted glare
Of trees and houses tightly locked, we tell
Each other once again: our oneness twice
The magnitude of one. And in our lair
Where darkenings deceive and quickly quell
The interloper light, our thighs suffice.

The Poet

Nine trying times had he performed
The feat of passion, raising somehow quickened
Blood: his poet heart was tough, but soft
Enough to keep his sacred marriage vow.

Poets have their never-ending grief:
A rusted apple, the rattle of a brittle leaf.
His tongue could feel the hardness of his teeth
Set like a bit that chafed inside his mouth
As he watched the idle boys sipping drinks
Upon their pedestals, thigh locked on thigh.

But he would talk of reeling into rich hotels,
Arms swelling with red-cheeked chicks ready
To ravage him to bits. These wish-sorties
He always travelled aloud when surrounded closely
By a crowd of sympathetic youthful writers
Whose low concurring cries drowned out the hollow
Echoes tolling behind the Poet's eyes.

Only ancient Greeks in simple dual
Disguise could translate love or pain by acts
Transcending the wooden face. The tearless poet
Wears his mask three thousand years too late.

ELEGY FOR MY FATHER

You lived remembering how your father
died (your hands were dry as leaves)
you talked about the hundred miners
lost when some tired cave
had heaved a heavy sigh, or the gardener
suddenly bolted with angina;
then some flavor filled your voice,
your decaying hands tremolo with that slow
disease of cells surrendering. Sometimes
you would simply nod your head like a metronome
to rhythms none of us could hear.

After dark, the last remains
of dinner borne away, you would
transplant yourself to a more receptive
chair and stare in quiet at the burned-out
fireplace. Only the tapping of plates
was heard, like the sound of distant workmen
with picks, loosening the ground.

Mother Among the Philodendra

—✦—

She found the trusted leaves predictable
if culled with favor, and so she offered
sustenance to those many tongues
inhabiting the dust. The vines
hung in silence, a kind of green
unknown beyond the ripening of leaves.

They spread out languorous upon lagoons
of tables as she tended her garden of Babylon.
On certain days she would replace
a limp ingrate that draped like weed;
they gave her room a jungle air,
the furniture would stare like hidden gimlet
eyes peering from underneath.

No one could disrupt the sucking
interlude of water-sifting earth.
Children were sealed away in distant
rooms, telling themselves tall
tales; little boys were idly
lifting toys and blocks, reedy
fingers locked from sight and sound.

She would feed and bathe the silent tendrils
hanging defenseless in the dark
and murmur of stricken beauty
beyond the riot of talk.

The Children

Here apostles
of my sleep
lie like dry debris
among the quilts and sheets;
So brief
they breathe
their slight mobility belies
the thunder underneath.
Eyes
that see their dreams
yet do not see,
hollow, staring out
like marble bas relief.
How they seem to speak
behind their
slender guise,
as blind men surrender:
parted lips,
palms upraised
for kindliness or alms.
Soon the sun's pink blood
transfuses them awake,
and they will not recall
the time

they could not see,
nor will believe,
as I,
apocrypha of dreams.

GENE POOL

He loves mankind but has contempt for man,
Abstraction feeds on those he cannot see;
His heart, though full, will readily expand
To pity those who are not fully free.

Another man, his crusty counterpart,
Loves his circle but detests the mass;
For those unwashed he has no bleeding heart,
He'll waste no warmth on populations crass.

Each bias will in all their offspring burn,
A gift of one half truth and one half lie;
Like bursting buds and aging leaves that turn
Our heritage of blood will never die.

Locked inside a quivering pair of genes
Lie formulae for human-made machines.

The French Provincial Drawing Room

She sits among the ornaments of grief
Framed tightly by the pathos of her smile,
Her pale hands hold a linen handkerchief
Dampened with little tears that stay a while.

Her face is sharply delicate and sweet,
Her thin and yellow hair is neatly set,
The patent pointed shoes that grace her feet
Have matching fashions black as her regret.

But courage, as it can now soothes her brow,
Following on the pretty pencilled line,
Adds beauty of the soul to every bow,
Her head and shoulders straight on stoic spine.

The eulogy she wrote before his death
His mourners read with suckings of their breath.

I do not think of Death as so sublime
To whisper sweet endearments in his ear,
Or resolutely slip through locking time
Exhilarating as my day draws near.

Nor do I cringe at putting out the light,
Inviting in the darkness where I lie,
Not even if the surface of each night
Would be a skein to skirt me as I die.

I mine my fortune knowing well the vein
Will come to nothing as the gold spins out,
Though love for love is heavy with its pain
I burn gem-like despite despair and doubt.

Death is simpler than the thought of death,
Breath is harder than the loss of breath.

Requiem for Stuart McCarrell: 2001

I tried to be your friend so many times,
but as a Nelson Algren devotee
your taste ran more to looser, freer rhymes;
I was a member of the bourgeoisie.

once you left a poem on my chair,
a jeering piece about a smart salon
where you and I had read; you had a flair
for denigrating fakes, but you went on

to boil me in a pentameter of oil,
chuckling as the bubbles crackled fire;
your burning images were meant to spoil
this other poet's rhetorical desire.

this is a tribute, as anyone can see,
to you, a People's poet (or is it to me?)

Bury Me in the Rain

Bury me in the rain,
let it clutch the earth below,

let my spirit hear those grieved clichés
on the grave robbery ending my days
and the song of the sea and the wind as it plays

for I am ready to go.

Bury me in the rain,
where the punishment fits the crime,

For the marshy wet and the earthy turn
so cooling and soothing to swallow my urn,
the sun is for laughter that ends with a burn,

But rain is the tears of the time.

Bury me in the rain,
the watchless nights of the realm

are properly served by uncolored decor
where grayness befits obitual lore,
a case of finality lessening more,

the elements are the helm.

O, bury me in the rain,

Snow Fall

It looks so delicate and sweet
Falling its balletic way,
Pirouetting in the street,
Lightening the darkest day.

On and on it plays its part,
Tirelessly without a pause,
But inhumane, it has no heart,
And buries all our worldly flaws

Leading us to the final folly
In covering up our melancholy.

PAINTING IN AN ALE HOUSE

She has no feeling in the matter:
two creatures tug at bulbous breasts,
appear to feed on blood, since pap
can't tame unnameables like these.

Those too-round fountains that she bears
look unconvincing as the makers
of such simple stuff as milk;
strangely, it is her face that catches
out the eye: reflects a kind
of unconcern with the rampant scene
below her chin, the hue of sour
cheese instead of human skin.

No dismay nor any hint
of fear, not even pride defines
her flaccid mouth and eyes. She looks
out dead-faced toward the girls whose hair
hangs behind their existential
smiles, and watches boys who stare
with weekend disaffiliate air
at nothing they can see or hear.

The pound of music hums along
the flaking paint; the lady's sucklings
drain away all human blood.

Still Life with Sleep

—∞—

We move in a breaking up of silence,
sounds are little more than sibilance of sheets,
persimmon streaks lick the wooden floor.

Your skin is a world of noble causes,
my slightly open eyes can see
complex effects of breath.

If history repeats itself no
moment can surpass this quiet hour,
this camera-quick tableau
broken by the undulations of your breast.

Tomorrow is the simplest of ideas,
the weeks, the years are nothing more than artifacts,
crutches clacking on the stones
convincing us we live.

But locked here in this capsule
we are like the seasons past or diffused
as spray into the atmosphere,
while somewhere behind emerging leaves
amorphous days are waiting for their birth.

The Man Upstairs: 1964

No woman could affirm my manhood
socketed between my thighs
as this soft malingerer whose eyes
were lashed with sweet mascara. A bedroom
we perused, three intruders losing
sense in a perfume redolence
thick as the pall of tombs where gracious
corpses lie among their precious
jewels. Costume pins were set
with deadly reckoning inside a box;
nearby twin clocks mixed minutes
in a counterpoint of ticks; askew
upon its rack a red wig sat,
caught the pinkness of an onyx lamp;
a wall held photographs of slender
men coiffed with thick and curving
hair, each with an eyebrow raised
as if to hang a question on the air.

Clothes make the man: displayed
in closets were the silk brocades,
rows of satin shirts and negligees
to celebrate some visitation
or punctuate a candlelit soiree.

He did not look into our eyes,
smoking and puttering, stuttering
low replies to the stout hausfrau
agent who led us in and out.

We bade goodbye and thanked the shy
young man. Our footsteps, rustling flowered
carpeting upon the stair,
made sounds like harmless snakes seeking
safety in a winding glade.

SO MANY NATURAL LAWS

So many natural laws
between the sun and moon,
those ancient double stars
which help us make ends meet;
our friends who give us leave

For all our painful flaws,
who know that much too soon
we all bear ancient scars
as if some blood conceit
could grant us a reprieve;

The children who we wake
upon a summer day,
they wonder at our talk,
our voices sound so odd,
our looks seem so intent.

Brooding on mistakes
the agéd snarl or pray
and take a daily walk
along the grassy sod
in garments they were lent.

IMPRINTS

Once running souls along the beach
are whited silhouettes,
water lines the crooked landscape,
fills the rivulets;

Hissing brine reluctantly
recedes, its solace spent,
it soon returns to wash the warming
prints of discontent;

Oscillating fathoms far
beyond the undertow,
laden with their heavy burden
burgeoning below;

Specific graves for the all the wash
this planet overturns,
overhead the endless air,
beneath the lava burns.

GIFTS FOR ALL

They urged me on to take whatever I might want,
a shirt, perhaps, some ties. "He was just your size," they said,
"and what do the dead need after they are gone?"
Aunt Hattie's eyes were darkened pools, her large nose
porous without its powder that used to cling like cloth.

She had so much to give away, had travelled a lot:
she would stand erect by a deep closet filled with gifts,
ringed in by relatives who would do a delighted little dance
as she slowly withdrew from yards of tissue a garment or trinket
from Brazil or France. All the wide-eyed sister-birds
would twitch, anticipating how their wrists would jingle,
or their fingers droop extravagance of opal stones
or amethysts. Joe, the freshly dead companion
on these jaunts, would sit and drool drops of ooze
along his elongated pure Havanas, and watch.

Oh, he could easily recall the sauteed fish he ate
at some hotel where Latin gongs announced their dinner
served, at last, in halls hung with chandeliers
of fancy glass. Besides, he could provide insights
a Baedeker would miss: "We met the Parkers in a Barton shop"
he'd say, laboriously wheezing away, digesting still
his memory of steak a Frog chef had cooked to death.

And so Aunt Hattie stood again, looking wan,
passing out the remnants of a hundred half-remembered
trips to poor and anxious sisters looking on;
the aimless largesse of withered arms bore gifts for all.

I stood, meaning to turn away, refusing to take
the deadly spoils, to pick the drapings of old Joe's bones:
I was much too good and strong to steal his shroud, I thought.
But when I finally left, there was a hardly worn green tie
that hung like a vine or noose around my reluctant neck:
it was *perfect*, they said, against my suit of charcoal brown.

MEASURING

———

This is the measure of time:

some slight rustling
of an aging leaf

or birds' brief montage
against the light

or the heavy sea
turned silver
in the moonwash
of the night

or you and I asleep.

"We live between emergencies," you said,
the garments of disease, the still life death
remembering: once a sculptor kissed your knees;
you wept and fled. But he was old as fathers
and you a callow foreigner afraid of language,
the violet laughter of the newest plums.

Your lips were not as timorous in Rome,
you sat beneath Italian sun and thought
of France; in Paris, Italy was home; but now
you tasted unknown condiments and kisses'
aftermath of kisses, the stain of grapes
had lingered on your tongue. "What do we need
to be encumbered for?" I asked, and then
awaiting a reply I saw your eyes
marbleized with broken veins. Every
night you sat and watched through deadened lids
your mother dying, or held your sister's hand.
(Can Europe really teach us better why
we live? Your hair was wound around your head,
stocking feet were cold beneath your dress.)
You sang a low Italian song and talked
of love that lies so easy on the Continent,
in the air, elemental as the rose

or wine or crust of bread white and soft
inside. You did not run from quiet bones,
you seemed to hold your breath, then sang again.

The clock upon the stove had all the time
to kill; mothers will die no sooner than
they can. I watched your hands, your eyes closed
against the pink and shaded pall of lamps.

SPARKS

We tinker with our bits of time
and talk about the loss of rhyme,
mixing drinks and metaphors,
recalling years of useful wars
amid relentless tick and tock
of the tall and stolid antique clock
as waning flames reduce the fire
reminding us of our own desire;

We ruminate about the young
with silver studs upon the tongue,
of too much artificial light
which makes us long for black and white.

Inside the hearth the crumbling logs
suffuse the copper firedogs
and sprays of lovely sparks portend
our own beginning and our end.

Boston: 1961

—

Boston hulks displeasured on the Bay
And rats repair to where the refuse piles;
Sore-eyed brownstones weep their agéd grief,
Decay in common for their commonweal.

Winds are blowing up the Boston dust,
Scratch the tinted panes that violet-dye
The snow, scuff the cracking in the street:
The hobbled cobblestones in silence stay.

One day defenseless birds at common play
Were caught in alien storm that twisted 'round
Unnatural to Massachusetts ways;
Old ladies cried and wrinkled men had tapped
Their canes in anger when uncouth winds had snapped
Treespines from their trunks. But soon swanboats
Once again skulked among the memories
Where festive rats begat in the lagoon.

In Marlborough Street, among the careful webs
And faded rugs, a poet sleeps, most fit
By blood as watchman to the Pilgrim dank.

The river Charles is babbling at its bank.

SPIRIT

A Spirit moves me as i write,
come at last to feed my want;
but where was it hiding the other night
as i frowned and struggled, crabbed and gaunt
for just a phrase defining days
i've spent without a ghost to haunt
when all my mind and body burned
for quenching spirits but they spurned
my proffered hand as poised with pen
i tried to raise one once again?

Spirit, Spirit, bloodless ghost,
who's the fool who needs you most?

ARRIVAL

She really loved these two smooth youths
brought forth from marriage bed, yet something
beyond her maidenhead demise
also fought for life; cool
white sheets had received her frightened thighs:
was it the sudden surprise of pain?
Or echoes of girlish tittering
that bobbled about inside her head?

Oh, she learned all right about the cadence
count of lying down, the iris
blossom bursting crowned with cock-crow
sounds, legs like limp akimbo.

But soon the days began to fall
like dice upon their bed and board,
and boredom grew like dustballs forming
in neglected rooms. How bodies cloy
when spirit turns and sees itself
a piece of mind believed no longer.

Disenchantment brought her dreams
stillborn, pulses beat from habit;
the dread of loneliness beguiles
and we bear smiles as eggs to breakfast.

She wound down through countless nights
while out beyond the window's glare
youthful bodies sprung to love,
undone by spring, and she among
the chairs with arms upturned stood empty.
A kind of lust ran in her blood
for those resilient childless young,
the humdrum agony of month
humping slowly up to month.

The trees pontificated tears
in April, keeper of flowers-to-be.
(One can die before her birth
in this cauldron earth where grief abides.)
She smoothed the pleated organdy
dry as gooseflesh to her touch
and saw the sun's reflected drops
of water skidding across her eye.

Along the wet concrete children
sang in monotones, away
from school, or flicked at leaves that hung
precipitous from new-sprung vines.
A few moments more and sons would
saunter up the gravel walk
and talk in earnest tones to half-
attentive ears about the running
kids in class who smelled, as they,
of multicolored paint and chalk.

Woman was meant to hurt for love,
she thinks, touching furtively

their hair, from the first wild burst
of blood to the final sigh of birth.
Oh, these faces: petal cheeks
that press into my wanton soul,
their features not yet spoiled, lips
faintly parted, heads half cocked
to hear some distant melody
higher than our decibels
can reach. Oh, God, this is enough!

But longings have the warmth and weight
of organs beating beating time
to some arrangement pre-ordained.
Impatient dinner huffs, and doilies
form a perfect four-square round:
predestination has a mundane
sound, like tire treads upon
a croaking gravel drive and bloodless
lips that punt a jowl in greeting.

And still the April rain falls.
Tomorrow I shall go away
she says again, and dawn was there,
its minute light like a whispered dare
and birds batted the air like clumsy
beasts prehistoric and extinct:
a somewhat too-beseeching note
lay upon the mantelpiece.

And now she sleeps from place to place
to find herself wherever hid . . .

As children play their aimless games
grownups conquer as they please
in the rubble of dichotomies.

Chicago: 1966

———

Dimly through frenetic snow,
plying stilted buildings
and the streets below,
agonized by tons of trucks
and compact autos' animus,
stoic streetlamps stiffly glow.

Living better electrically
the fingers of the signs decree
in frippery of red and blue:
Dine, Dance, Bar-B-Q.

Beside the agitated lake
among the Gothics and the glass
a simple sentence makes a claim:
"9 out of 10 cook with gas!"

Parks are empty, harbors stare
through December's guttural air,
spastic wind berates the streets,
blots out windows that it meets,
dimming lights to wizened O's,
painting buildings as it goes.

Among the feathers of the snow
stoic streetlamps stiffly glow.

Turner's "Interior at Petworth"

Somewhere there is always the light,
A whirling dervish of gold,
Strong as God
Or the blinding blur of the cave.
You cannot turn away,
Eyes fixed onto the paint
That seems to spin with fire:
Objects of the real world lie,
Some bright, others merely gray,
All varied, they seem to say:

"Yes, we are reflections, but we are life."

Coming to Grips

Like every faceless fact that stares with zeal,
(Interrogator light's relentless beam),
Illiterate death reminds us we are real
And all events exactly as they seem.

The levity of spring that warmth begets,
Its disappearing act which yearly taunts
Our bubbling summer blood if it forgets
The colder courses honing in their haunts.

Look now upon this world as if a fool,
A smiling stranger idly telling time,
Remember no exception probes the rule
Of truth which houses reason without rhyme.

Then let illusion lead you where it may,
But shed its trappings as you make your way.

The Broken Clock

How odd to watch the time tick off
And yet to see it won't amass:
The second hand's persistent cough
Cannot make the minutes pass.

Stolidly at five o'clock
The timer hands both stiffly stand,
Held in an eternal lock,
Imprisoned in a timeless land.

How would it be to spend my time
And yet to keep it all in store?
I watch this hapless pantomime
And wonder which is less or more.

I think then of Tithonus' grief
Who ages but can never die;
This moving hand remains a thief,
The others rigid as they lie.

To the Luddites

If only you had won your holy war
We might not now be seething in our fight
With software reeling in their spastic lore
To find us, even where we sleep at night.

And yet all wars are fought to fight no more,
We make our lathes for turning burnished steels
To pile up monuments, and as before,
Our blood is lubricant to spinning wheels.

Still, your tiny numbers, your hopeless cause,
Though in their time mundane as labor strife,
Seem to us far seeing, like natural laws
Reaching into the core of every life.

If only you had won your holy war
It might have been that fight to fight no more.

LONDON SONG: 1967

The City sifts the mist,
The river shrugs away,
Like pursed lips unkissed
The skies forever gray.

>   Swing on, London,
>   Sing Big Ben,
>   The Embankment is a dungeon
>   In a shark-infested Thames.

Mini spirits driving
Keep left in the mind,
Workers all are striving
As work is left behind.

>   Swing on, London,
>   Sing Big Ben,
>   The Embankment is a dungeon
>   In a shark-infested Thames.

Undismissed the classes,
Has the war begun?
Soiled and sullen masses
Searching for the sun.

Swing on, London,
Sing Big Ben,
The Embankment is a dungeon
In a shark-infested Thames.

ODE TO THE NOT-YET-DEAD: 1972

Cell meets cell upon this looted world,
Asian wounded do their hideous dance,
Decent folks are moved by flags unfurled,
Children stamp their feet in dusty camps.

Music plumbs the acres deep and wide,
Pine and pine, they also stand and wait,
Skin's but skin on those who will have died,
Concert for the mass to lie in state.

Simple, subtle sounds, the cymbals bite,
Firelight on the hearth, the paddies glare,
Legions lead us on to splendid fight,
Smells of hope and death affright the air.

The living kill the living and we try
To make such pretty noises as they die.

When I Die

Every solitary bird will sing
A mournful song for the solace it may bring,
Clots of teeming bees will halt their honeying,
Grapes hang heavier from the vines to which they cling.

Harrumphing seas will all the greater swell,
Thick trees will flex their prisoned roots to tell
The nether things what's up above their hell,
The earth awash in church-spires' somber knell.

Oh, yes, the world will surely be awry,
Never to be the same the day I die.

PRAY FOR PEACE

Pray for peace,
Lift up your hollow throats
And pray for peace,
While doves coo their mating hurt,
Warm eggs bubble within their lime
And great minds meet in a single thought.

Pray for peace,
The blood is swelled in rounded veins,
Cold rain shivers in the eye
And trees stuck in teeming mud
Wave a last goodbye.

THE KOZY KORNER MOTEL

Easy, the franchise-man had said,
smiling as he held their hands,
enveloping them in his glow
and the musk of his cologne.
And now they wait for custom,
not so far off the beaten track;
they can even hear the distant
swish of cars plummeting along
the highway. Only six months. Easy.

Here comes a dark-haired young man,
clutching a small valise, a bookman,
a traveller, a solid citizen
whose route he will repeat.
"Just one night?" she says.
"One night," her husband says.
"Yes, one night," he says. "This time."
They smile. He retires.

The dark descends;
they do not dare to search
each other's faces overlong.

"Good morning," she says, "sleep well?"
"Yes," he replies, calling up
in his head the flat, slate-grey
paint and the narrow iron bed.

"You made," her husband says,
"a hundred calls!"
The startled guest catches his breath.
"Oh, no! Only five, I'm afraid . . ."
holding his plastic card aloft.
"On this."
The silence is broken only by
the register's crickety voice.
(Who made those hundred calls?
Who dreamed them up?
Whose nightmare is this, anyway?)

"Thank you," she says, "come again."
"Oh, yes."
The office door closes
gently behind him.

Easy is the rain
dotting all the leaves,
easy is the grass
bending to the breeze.

REALIST (   )

—∞—

I have seen the cruel blue threats of dawn,

As Nature,
Blatant at its worst
Flaunts its beauty at me first,
As if I'm fool enough think
Benignly at the sight of pink.

(Not me. I know the clay it shines upon.)

Color kindly helps the earth deceive,

With darkest umbrage cuts the glare
Of objects' hardness and we stare
In flaccid wonder at the turn
Of leaves that simply dry and burn.

(But I'm no fool. I know what to believe.)

The grass deports in regimental green,

As randomly the earth below
Belies the order of the snow

And variations of events
Lend a logic to our sense.

(But still I say: distrust what you have seen.)

WINTER

—◦—

Winter blew it all night long
Chuckling coldly in the breeze,
Sungold sung its ancient song:
Ruined fortunes of the trees
Played the day's disharmonies.

Puffing with insidious pride,
Feckless, hollow all inside,
Wilder now that night has died,
Gales of laughter echoing wide.

Taking brazen liberties
Is part of winter's icy blight,
Flaunting incivilities,
Taunting childlike in the night:
Reasoning is put to flight.

Winters go and winters come,
Winter's substance is the sum.

Killing the Winter Was Our Cause

Killing the winter was our cause,
twice our love, was wisely spent
as wind tongued its way along the window,
ill-begotten, icy its intent.

But we could afford to be beneficent,
moving together like summer-heated rivers,
we had no need to curse the elements.

Bales of indifferent snow
floated by our pane,
the gale became resigned to our content,
we heard its distant wail,
and turning ever slightly once again,
our tongues began to stir
the mistral in our veins.

BARTER

—※—

Now the winter seems a pseudonym
for some disparagement of blood,
hymnal of the snow a requiem
mourning for the absent birds.

In the veins unceasing marathon
slender as the April rain,
cold remains of winters newly gone
parse redundancies of days.

Sleep contorts the daily epitaph
dotted on telegraphy of nerve,
death's a figure on a paper graph
or thin destruction of a word.

Come, seasons, do your maximum,
be true to life in anger or in calm,
strike our deaf-mute eyes till we are numb,
we possess the promise of the worm.

After a Black "Abstract Painting"

If nothing's ever really what it seems,
Phenomena dissect phenomena,
Understanding makes a fool of us
And all reality is left to dreams.

Even cameras' objective eyes
Cannot hope to shutter in the truth,
Revealing what our vision is denied;
Human insight is a web of lies.

But do not think that abstract painters play
With our own frailty and defenselessness:
Once again at blackness look and see
A cross, when neon shines a certain way.

CARNEY

Here lies Carney
underneath the plastered rock,
where rain rolls tepid
in the summer heat,
ices its temper
in December frost.

Here lies Carney (W.J.)
with a rosary draped
where his neck once lay,
hugging the moss
on standing stones,
holding the line
on his sifting bones.

Here lies Carney
whose soul has gone to meet
the nameless friars kissing
countless dirty feet.

TRILOGY FOR A FRIEND WHO TOOK TO HIS BED

I
HIMSELF

I cannot count the many months and years
That I have lain alone inside this room;
All talk has stopped, no more bitter tears,
No doctors to invade my private tomb.

The steady dripping of the autumn rain
Against the pure white wooden eaves;
Coded messages rap the window pane,
Spell out their secrets on the fallen leaves.

She comes just now, bearing a metal tray
And sets it softly on the table by
My bed and waits in silence for me to say
What I always say: "Thank you" and "Goodbye."

She turns and exits, closing the door behind;
Even now she doesn't seem to know
What motives clot the facets of my mind;
I see that she still hopes and will not go.

What can I say to her? "My dear, my life
Is ludicrous and I'm an empty shell
And your indulgence as my wedded wife
Somehow eases this long-living hell."

Which would of course be a blatant lie;
How could I be so cruel to tell the truth?
If only she would simply let me die
With memories of my now long-distant youth

When I solemnly agreed to plot the lines
Of melodies the crooked branches play
And score the music of the twisted vines,
Note what the crumbling boulders have to say.

This long commitment I have sworn to keep
Above all others; she will never know
These many thousand nights I do not sleep
What must be done till the very day I go.

II
His Wife

Once again I wish him dead
And yet remain his loyal wife;
He lies immobile on his bed
A refugee from daily life.

I bite my tongue to spike the curse
As I have done for thirty years,
And acting as his faithful nurse
Provided comfort through my tears.

Robotically I bear a tray,
A ritual in sacrifice;
I feed my habit every day,
An addict locked inside a vise.

His bed is very like a grave
Or frame that could well be his bier;
His room is dank as any cave
And though he breathes his death is here.

I leave my nightly offering
To feed him and assuage my guilt;
He thanks me for the food I bring
And stiffly lies beneath his quilt.

The carpet hisses at the wood
When I shut the heavy bedroom door
As if to mock the little good
I've done a thousand times before.

The sun clings to the highest hill
As it retreats from autumn skies;
Its lingering light is heated still
And yet, at last, thank God it dies.

III
His Son

My father curls up in his bed
And makes believe that he is dead.

Twenty years ago and more
And I remember still,
We wrung our hands and paced the floor:
How could we break his will?

The doctors came, the doctors went
With newest therapies,
But none of them proved heaven sent,
Could not provide surcease.

My father curls up in his bed
With fervent wishes he was dead.

My only sibling cried and cried
And even tried to pray
As if he had already died,
Her face was cold and gray.

My mother, stoical and calm,
Still coming at his beck and call,
Offers every sort of balm;
He stares unseeing at the wall.

My father curls up in his bed
And will not die till we are dead.

High Mindedness

—⟩⟩⟨⟨—

A poet who's been burned looks down
at his Dalmatian hand,
his heart and mind are convoluted
as an ampersand;
Truth transcendent he might seek
to set his standards by,
Although his thoughts are seldom ever
more than hipster high.

THE SEVENTH DAY

Somewhere outside our window we hear the ponder
bells and rest our heads upon a pillow;
we lie with smiles that swell inside our bones,
cathedral of our blood-enfolding heart.

I pray for you this morning in our house
softened with the noise of slippered feet
and distant little boys: the open window
frames a sprig of leaves. The bells toll
for us, their iron tongues beseech in monotones,
we find our solace turning each to each.

MERRY CHRISTMAS

Santas wring the peace for our salvation,
Sluices clatter with your borrowed gold,
Effigies have feelings and foundations
Shake down like flesh that begs out in the cold.

Dimmest, distant sounds are hard of hearing,
Way down inside you know your bones are soft,
Since the day of reckoning is nearing,
We send our latest bill of goods aloft.

Ordinary snow that freezes solid,
The stamping boots that beat the season up,
Red for cheer to elevate the squalid,
Cold draughts to aid our spending as we sup.

And so the Holy story Love and Light
Will rest again to sleep till Christmas night.

VIGIL

Our talk was quiet as an autumn vesper
whispered under hollow spire,
whited candles surrendered to fire.

How love consumes us in this occult way,
unceremonious lights falter
once or twice, convulse but stay.

Some say the end is the beginning
and play with flame already tenuous
as ghosts or half-hearted jokes.

But we press on and only stir
to hold our breath and watch with tense
and burning eyes the wax wane.

OUR FATHER,

---

which heaven art thou in
that thou canst touch me from within?
thy unkissed lips can only meet
to bless the vicar of thy speech;

and how do the souls of the rosebuds dwell
Among the vapors of thy hell?
canst thou predict how gardens grow
or stop the journeys of the snow?

who can pause to listen now
to broken monologues of how
thou tried to love, could only feel
the chastening of tempers' steel?

who will listen, who abide?
no one, father, only I.

Awakening

—∞—

Laughter ends the beleaguered night
Though sleep had been my wish,
There were beggars for horses beyond the light,
I endlessly halved a fish.

What a relief that symbols die
At the sight of a parchment shade,
God's in the world at my opening eye
And ghosts are heavenly laid.

STARTLED

A startled sparrow startled me
and nearly grazed my balding head,
it darted from a maple tree
and seemed to tremble as it fled.

I quickly mused: so much like me,
turning away from the evening gloom
when shadows hover on the lea
outside the comfort of my room.

The chain of being will ply its term
all along our fretful span,
I'd like to tell the earthy worm:
your fate's no worse than that of man.

Cemetery

White geese roam the meadow,

far off the cockatoo moans,
wind blows, thin dust rolls
and lives a while
in the shallow
script of stones
blind upon the hills.

Alone the fastened grass,
the hard-bit soil shifts
and sifts the bones.

(Green grow the rushes ho)

AFTERMATH

Measuring all things as a man,
my proper study or your woman's attitude
moves us even closer than our bodies can,
lying loosely as two lovers would.

The climate of our bed is warm
(small world this cubicle),
pillows for our heads
have long ceased to be of use.

Unaccustomed to a public speech
and even less to craft of privacy,
we reach for one another's mouths to feel,
our words as muted as our docile sheets.

Unseen, the night comes down,
we move into parabolas of sleep
and dream of waking wordlessly at dawn,
remind the sun of promises to keep.

The Satyrs

Going from bed to verse
among the lightning days
or nights' intensity,
he looked upon his rhymes
as graves to lie in
while sitting upright
as a banker in his chair;
his bed was all he had
to keep himself alive.

Too much thought beguiles;
the spectre with the empty throat
smiles a mischievous smile,
tasting torture in his satyr's way,
more satisfied to watch a poet writhe
than kiss his life away.

For his part
the poet plays the game,
wise as any man
who sees the signs of death,
and writing off his pain
takes love to bed again.

In the wings
the vacant vampire waits
and marks the time.

Her Pleasure

Across the pattern of her face
lines as fine as those on old Limoges
break into a smile.

Her features designate
the time and place for mirth,
a sudden birth of anger
tends the craters of her eyes.

Her mouth does not need
buffooneries of speech
to indicate she's pleased or piqued.

One's fortune bides its time
to nervously declaim
inside the harbor of her gaze,
her sights graze above her bosom
oversize as glacial burdens left behind.

Sunshine or epileptic rain
wait upon the seasons of her mind.

Beneath the Bottom

—✺—

Surrounded by rivulets of graying weeds
precocities of flowers play alive;
vapid pansies bathe in velveteen,
the iris hides an indecisive smile;
grass is long and languorous in green
and proud to be so populous a fleet.

The mildest March we've known contritely blows
emancipated lilies in the pond,
the frog, presumptuous about the calm,
disturbs the stems whose roots are far below.

The frost will come to bleed the roses white,
too soon the buds surrender maidenheads;
who wakens obese bees to hone the sky,
who splits the tender seedling overnight?

Self Portrait

Outside this cylinder of skin
light and shadow shutter past,
only can the camera clasp
some indecisive wave or fear.

I see myself as others see me
in this photograph:
too little hair, too little chin,
crow's feet webbing weaving in.

Too bad Heraclitus lived too soon,
not knowing how we've civilized,
watching our locked faces self-
assured, smiling or surprise.

A fortune waits upon our immortality
to see what we have been (or are),
a moment's life imprisonment
behind the bar of gloss
that leers and leers or frowns

Looking at me as I am,
as others never really know,
who might admire or be amused
at the picture's pose,

I recognize a fraction of myself
white the whole man gropes
in my homily of blood,
a ghost unknown.

I turn to watch a tree
stroke the seasoned sky
and see that birds know my kind:
they roost, cooing, at my window.

Wind Chimes

Baser metals can't transmute to gold
nor frozen tones achieve a melody,
adversarial winds blow hot and cold
inviting tides of fruitless alchemy.

Burnished tubes are dancing marionettes
which stand like priests in garb, their heads secure,
they dandle, swing and clang in rigid sets
when urged to move by ghostly forces pure.

Relentlessly these cipher voices toll,
rankling like the mindless crush of glass,
their pleasant-cruel refrain reminds my soul
how swift and bitter all these moments pass.

These voluble and hard-nosed zealots play
while humans agonize our lives away.

Deconstruction

Because I must fixate on rhyme
I try to sew my seems,
belaboring a hundredth time
to place the structure's beams
in parallels and one by one
to make the neatest rows,
when suddenly they come undone
like cold and trackless floes.

Once more, I say, unto the breach,
to battle with my scrawl,
my grasp must not exceed my reach
or nothing's built at all.

So I will stick it to the last,
see what the lines portend,
until the die is finally cast
and I've no more to spend.

In the Balance

It's gravity, you see, that pulls a person down,
Your original weight's enough to make you make
Mistakes. (Of course no judgment meant.) Around
She goes and where she stops is where you take

Your turn, that's that. But this is the land of the living,
And those who make their way by making plans
Crammed with storing up and never giving
A damn or even a cent to empty hands

Are dead already. But what of all the rest
Of earth's beating things, each with loads
To cripple golden intents? The very best
Of us can't not wonder. Each logic goads.

Oh, Heavenly Father, Who calls us ever up,
Your heavy bounty's tempest in our cup.

Special Needs

I need some thunder on this burden day
And shocks of lightning parsing jagged thoughts;
Instead, I hear desultory drops
Of half-hearted, indifferent, softest rain.

No, this will not do. I cannot deal
With compromise when feelings are at stake:
Dividing spoils, that kind of give and take
Is well enough for what we buy, or steal.

But art needs something nearer still to fire,
The sodden smoldering of a choked restraint
Must burst to color like sudden flung paint
Or die aborning in its knot desire.

Give that man a cigar! He has the answer:
He does not want the dance, he wants the dancer.

HOMO SAPIENS

—◆—

Slightly lower than the arachnid
On a scale of species classified,
Ego overwhelmed by Super Id,
Personality is calcified.

Why do his decisions emphasize
Flinty processes electrical,
Turn capacities to sympathize
Into actions asymmetrical?

Why indeed does manliness involve
Kinds of blindness only he contracts?
Complex qualities whose roots devolve
Onto veins by which his brain reacts.

Take a powder, child, and mix with milk,
Sow the ears with finer lines than silk.

WILL

I'm not myself today (nor any other),
My marrow's crammed with foreign agent cells
Conspiring day and night with one another
To lock my spirit in if it rebels.

But what good's fealty felt through such constraint?
A soldier's marching orders, dutibound;
Do painters' dictates lie beyond the paint
Or singers' songs transcend the merely sound?

And yet although I know the form is cast
By now so long suited to a pattern laid
My own years ago (and fit to last),
I think, I am whatever I've been made.

Common senses kindly let me see
That knowledge makes me wise if never free.

WHAT NEXT?

Call it music if you will,
Cacaphonies of crowds of crows
Filter past my window sill,
What they're saying no one knows.

Are they heralding the light?
Or saddened by departing night?

They cannot say such simple things,
Flapping 'round the stolid trees,
Floating on their liquid wings,
Rousting squirrels, honey bees.

Such a fuss about a sun,
Something new and something done.

Bequest

From head to toe I know the bladed grass
That cuts my vision every working day;
My nights are filled with monumental dreams,
I bless the sun that washes them away.

The rooted problem slowly seems to fade
As ticket takers smile and let me pass,
Persistent wheels are turning on their rails,
My berth secure behind a double glass.

The heady hazard of the city streets,
The little that I do, so much is said;
The hoot and trump of business meeting minds,
While lurking in the dark my buried bed.

I live because I die, and so I give
Whatever I become to those who live.

About the Author

Jordan Miller earned his MA in English at the University of Illinois at Chicago. He founded The Poetry Seminar in 1959, where poets met to critique one another's work. The group also sponsored readings in Chicago by e.e. cummings, Robert Lowell, Howard Nemerov, and other poets. Mr. Miller was a founding editor of *Choice*, a journal of poetry. His work has appeared in a number of literary publications. He is also the author of *Letters from Prague*, a play.